Presented to

_____

by

_____

on

_____

DEVOTIONS FOR NEW MOMS

RUTH TUTTLE CONARD

Harold Shaw Publishers
Wheaton, Illinois

Unless otherwise indicated, all Scripture quotations are taken from *The Holy Bible, New International Version.* Copyright © 1973, 1978, 1984 International Bible Society. Used by permission of Zondervan Publishing House. All rights reserved.

Scripture quotations marked CEV are from *The Contemporary English Version* of the Bible.

Scriptures marked TLB are taken from *The Living Bible,* © 1971, and are used by permission of Tyndale House Publishers, Inc., Wheaton, IL 60189. All rights reserved.

Scripture quotations marked *The Message* are from *The Message.* Copyright © 1993, 1994, 1995 by Eugene H. Peterson. Used by permission of NavPress Publishing Group.

Cover design by David LaPlaca.

ISBN 0-87788-172-3

Library of Congress Cataloging-in-Publication Data

Conard, Ruth, 1942-
    Devotions for new moms / Ruth Conard.
        p.   cm.
     ISBN 0-87788-172-3
     1. Mothers—Prayer-books and devotions—English.   I. Title.
 BV4847.C66 1996
 242'.6431—dc20   95-3432
                                                                CIP

---

02 01 00 99 98 97 96

10 9 8 7 6 5 4 3 2

To my daughter
Melody Ruth
who dared to believe that God would provide
for her and her baby . . .

and

for the multitude of women who share that belief.

Preface

*I*n the early autumn of 1969, our family of four sat in the morning worship service of a small southern California church. On my lap our seventeen-month-old son put his rubber Mr. Gumbie through a workout while his three-year-old sister leaned comfortably against her daddy's side. In my womb nestled our third child.

The preacher was well into Matthew 24, the second coming of Jesus Christ. But my mind strayed from the coming of my Lord to the going of his servants—in this instance, my husband and me—going back as missionaries to Peru, South America, where our new baby would be born.

My mind was engulfed with the hows, whens, and wheres of these events. When would money actually be available to get on that plane? How far along would I be in my pregnancy? Would I like my new doctor there? Where would I deliver? And how would I ever manage *three* small children when their father preached on Sundays? (Nurseries were unheard of in that part of the world, and *pampers* was only a verb referring to one's possible treatment of a child!) It was so hard to focus on a future event when the weight in my own body, combined with two little wiggly people outside my body, focused me on the present.

Skipping down the page of Scripture, playing catch-up with the preacher, verses 19 and 20 grabbed my attention. I sucked in my breath: Jesus, my Lord, was speaking two thousand years ago, privately to his disciples, and he said (referring to the fall of Jerusalem forty years into the future), "How dreadful it will be in those days for pregnant women and nursing mothers! Pray that your flight will not take place in winter or on the Sabbath."

I was amazed, comforted, overjoyed, and filled with hope by these thoughtful, compassionate words of my Creator regarding a very vulnerable, special section of society: pregnant women and nursing mothers! I had never heard nor seen a news commentary nor read a news magazine in which anyone in power—king, queen, president, or dictator—had ever murmured even a hint of concern for this select group during times of national or international disaster. Nor were these words commented on by the preacher that morning.

But here was Jesus Christ, Creator of the universe, Lord of the nations, King of kings, bending down across space and time to whisper to me beautiful and strengthening words: "Ruth, I am very aware of you in this instant; that you are a pregnant woman, a soon-to-be nursing mother. I love you and the four on this pew so close to your heart. I understand you and will care for you. Be at peace, my daughter."

That is why this devotional is written for you, a new mother: with a prayer that you bond anew with your God in this new phase of life, sensing his love and strength as you consider the scriptural stories of godly women and men before you who birthed and nurtured life, asked questions, voiced complaints, reflected deeply, and allowed their faith to be stretched, enabled by the living God.

I often wished for a book like this as I traveled the backroads of Peru, mothering three little ones. Enjoy!

Note to the reader: Some questions in the "reflecting" section suggest that you write responses or thoughts in a personal notebook or journal. If you don't already have one, you might want to purchase a small notebook to use especially for recording your reflections on these devotions.

Leading You Gently

He tends his flock like a shepherd: He gathers the lambs in his arms and carries them close to his heart; he gently leads those that have young.

Isaiah 40:11

Life seems to spiral down to *gentleness* when that tiny bundle is placed in your arms. You don't feel like rushing around (frankly, you can't!) nor talking loud, nor making abrupt movements. No, every inner body signal seems to flash, "Gentle, please be gentle." Someone uniquely new and fragile lies next to you, snuggles at your breast, breathes ever so softly against your neck.

Most women long for gentleness from those around them in this hour of life. Many worries crowd in. Will I ever lose this weight? Will I ever have the energy and desire for sexual intimacy with my husband again? When will I be able to keep to a schedule? When will I not be sleepy? How will we find the money for all that's ahead of us? When will my emotions level out?

In the Bible we are pictured as sheep. And Jesus says that he is the Good Shepherd. He says that in his goodness, he knows you, and he knows your name. He came to give you an abundantly full life, even unending, eternal life. All of those thoughts can fill you with joy and hope. However, there is one part of his shepherding which is uniquely applicable to you as a new mom. Jesus is not scolding you. He is not pushing or pulling you. He is not making demands on you, nor glaring at you with heavy expectations.

No, Jesus, the Lamb of God, walks beside you today, gently guiding you in the newness of your daily routine. With him beside you, you will not have to fend for yourself or try to be more than you are. For Jesus, your gentle shepherd, is leading you gently.

Reflecting

1. What is the greatest worry on your mind today? Ask God to give you the courage to share your concern with a person close to you.
2. Watch for evidence of God's gentle leading in your life today. Jot it down in your journal at the end of the day.

Praying

"Gentle Shepherd, come and lead me,
  For I need You to help me find my way.
Gentle Shepherd, come and feed me,
  For I need Your strength from day to day."*

* From "Gentle Shepherd." Words by Gloria Gaither. Music by William J. Gaither. Copyright ©1974 William J. Gaither. Used by permission.

Seeking Nourishment

Long to grow up into the fullness of your salvation; cry for this as a baby cries for his milk.

1 Peter 2:3, TLB

*W*e take many things for granted about newborns. For example, the sucking instinct. Every newborn knows how to nurse, right? Wrong.

Not long ago, a new mom called me from the hospital birthing room. She was frustrated trying to get her one-day-old baby to nurse. Even his cries for nourishment seemed halfhearted. You can imagine the tension and guilt this new mom experienced, not to mention her physical discomfort. Finally doctors determined that a hole in the heart depleted the baby's strength, even the strength to cry for what he needed. When he was three months old, the hole was repaired.

During this special time, your little one's desire for milk can be a spiritual object lesson. How many times a day does she cry for milk? Through what stages of anxiety does she pass before being quieted? Do your attempts quiet her? Why? How?

Is there any similarity between the newborn's desire for milk and your desire for God? Healthy babies want lots of milk and at times want it as often as they can get it! This is a natural time for you to sense a renewed longing to know your Creator. After all, the baby you hold has so recently come from him. As one writer has said, "God is on the inside of our longing."

In other words, when you feel a longing for God, it is really God himself longing for you!

However exciting and/or exhausting this phase of your motherhood is, seek to grow up more in your life with God. For most, that cannot possibly mean deep, prolonged Bible study and prayer. Most new moms would slide straight out of the chair in an asleep heap on the floor! Rather, seek him with your heart in the quiet moments of feeding your baby. A quiet praise tape may help you along. As your baby rests, take a few moments to rest your cares in God's hands. Rejoice in his forgiveness and cleansing as you bathe your newborn. You will be walking toward the accomplishment of 1 Peter 2:3.

Reflecting

1. What could you do during your few quiet times (either with or without the baby) to help you focus on God and grow in your love for him?
2. Ask a woman you admire, one who has passed through this phase of life, for any creative ideas she employed to keep seeking after God while mothering in the early stages.

Praying

Loving God, thank you for this beautiful analogy of how I am to seek after you. Please give me a desire to be nourished by you that is as intense as my baby's desire to be nourished by me.

Treasured Moments

But Mary treasured up all these things and pondered them in her heart.

Luke 2:19

*M*ary didn't have a television, and she didn't have a telephone to occupy her time. Imagine!

But she did have what really counts—a heart for God and his will, a desire to reflect, and a sense that something big was taking place, of which she was a part. She didn't treat lightly her circumstances or the people surrounding her: the appearance of angels, the comfort of cousin Elizabeth graced with prophetic words, the song given her by God in Elizabeth's presence, the bare stable surroundings, the loving care of Joseph, the visit of the shepherds and their account of the angelic choir. She thought about these things often, and they were a treasure to her.

These treasures of God's intimate closeness during her time of pregnancy and birthing undoubtedly sustained Mary in later years, as she accompanied her firstborn son, Jesus, through life (though with a mother's questions, fears, and grief) to the cross and beyond.

Yes, and beyond. Beyond to the glorious resurrection, Jesus' ascension into heaven, and her participation with all the disciples in prayer and in the filling by the Holy Spirit!

Reflecting

1. You have begun a new part of life. What events surrounding the birth of your baby are treasures to you?
2. In your baby book or journal, write down those blessings of God surrounding this precious, life-changing event. Include thoughts, observations, and feelings—anything you are seeing and sensing at this time.
3. List those specific people who have been special to you during these months.

Praying

Loving Creator, I thank you for the *treasures* you have given me throughout these special months of life. May I not take them for granted, but rather see the events, people, and circumstances as all given by you, a loving God. Help me to occupy my time well, so that these months will be good stepping stones toward future events.

From Pain to Joy

A woman giving birth to a child has pain because her time has come; but when her baby is born she forgets the anguish because of her joy that a child is born into the world.

John 16:21

I am surrounded by young women in my workplace. Last week one of them experienced a very difficult Caesarean section. Fear, pain, and improper administration of anesthesia combined to create a traumatic birth. However, two weeks earlier, another colleague delivered her first baby, experiencing a total of only two hours of labor.

Every birthing story is different. While the process may be the same, each individual experience is truly unique. During labor for our first child, which seemed eternally long, I remember whispering to my husband, "Let's not do this again."

During labor for our second child, in less than ideal circumstances, I remember groaning to my husband, "Let's not do this again." And yet two years later a third child was born, again with my full cooperation and consent. Obviously the joy of holding a newborn child in my arms was greater than the anguish by which it came!

Reflecting

1. In your journal, write down what you always want to remember from your birthing experience. What was positive? What was negative? Which do you think you will most remember and recount?
2. In what ways were you helped through any anguish?
3. Do you find any of the painful aspects of birthing diminishing in your mind? Why do you think that is happening?
4. Perhaps nothing worthwhile in life is birthed without pain. If you find that statement true, describe another experience in your life that in some way paralleled the experience of birthing, a time when you experienced agony, but great joy and satisfaction came about in the end.

Praying

Great Comforter, thank you for the strength and courage to birth my baby. And I thank you so much for the joy I am experiencing now with my baby in my arms. I praise you today.

Words of Faith

Adam lay with his wife Eve, and she became pregnant and gave birth to Cain. She said, "With the help of the LORD I have brought forth a man!" Later she gave birth to his brother Abel.

Genesis 4:1-2

*H*ave you ever considered these words spoken by Eve, "mother of all the living," ancient mother of you and me? We have no written record of any spoken words by Adam after Genesis 3. But Eve is quoted twice in chapter 4. In both cases (4:1 and 4:25) her words are recorded after birthing events.

Here we see Eve's inner fiber and faith. Amazing, really, when you consider how alone she was and how new this whole process of pregnancy and birthing was. In many cultures of the world a woman is considered alone if another woman is not present. A husband or children do not count. People belonging to those cultures believe that a woman needs another woman beside her—for female camaraderie, help, and sometimes for protection. Eve had no mother, no sister, no aunts nor grandmother nearby; no female friend. She had never even *seen* another woman! She had to forgo the privilege of any Lamaze classes and had not *one* "how-to" book in her possession. And yet her words do not reflect a sense of loneliness. Rather, they are words of wisdom, truth, and trust.

They are, astoundingly, words of the very first *created* woman upon delivering the first *born* human! She did not cry, "Whoa, what pain!" or "Believe me, I'll never go through *that* again!" She recognized that the God with whom she had walked in the Garden continued to walk with her even now, in the world outside that Garden. And so she exclaims with passionate faith, "With the *help of the Lord* I have brought forth a man." And later, *"God* has granted me another child." There was no doubt in the mind of our ancient mother Eve—creation involves three, not just two: God, woman, and man.

Reflecting

1. Getting past the pain of labor, what were your first thoughts and/or words upon seeing your baby?
2. How did you sense the Creator God's involvement in the birth of this child?

Praying

Loving God, I praise you that you are . . .
Loving God, I thank you for . . .
Loving God, I ask you that . . .

God: Wise Creator

You knit me together in my mother's womb. . . . I am fearfully and wonderfully made. . . . My frame was not hidden from you when I was made in the secret place. When I was woven together in the depths of the earth, your eyes saw my unformed body.

Psalm 139:13-16

*Y*ou've looked that little body over again and again for flaws, birthmarks, or skin eruptions, haven't you? How many of us moms, upon first surveillance, found a minature ear doubled over and thought our precious new one was deformed for life!

According to Psalm 139, God was watching over the formation of your baby long before she was felt by you. Your baby's character and personality, assets and liabilities, strengths and weaknesses are all known completely by her loving Creator. What a relief! The One who chose to create this new life knows her intimately.

He knows her so well, in fact, that he has already designed the frame around the picture of her life. He has established the parameters, the length of life for her. He knows what she can sustain. And within that frame of life, her Creator will never leave her nor abandon her as she learns to lift her voice to him.

What an intriguing role you have been given—to walk beside her as her mother, guiding her in the discovery of the One who formed her, watching her first movements of praise to him, reading to her about his wonderful works, and affirming her in the knowledge that she is *indeed* fearfully and wonderfully made. How long will it take you to discover all that the Lord has fashioned into this one little girl? Probably . . . a lifetime.

Reflecting

1. Write down the names of women in your life who have been like mothers to you, guiding and leading you in your knowing of God. Beside each name, write what you have appreciated about each one.
2. What would you like to imitate from these women as you mother your child?

Praying

Today, make Psalm 139:13-16 your own prayer: "Dear Loving God, thank you for creating my daughter's inmost being; for knitting her together in my womb. I praise you because she is fearfully and wonderfully made; your works are wonderful, I know that full well. Her frame was not hidden from you when she was made in the secret place. When she was woven together in the depths of the earth, your eyes saw her unformed body. All the days ordained for her were written in your book before one of them came to be. And today, God, these truths quiet me and give me great hope for her. Thank you."

Celebrating with Others

By now Elizabeth's waiting was over, for the time had come for the baby to be born—and it was a boy. The word spread quickly to her neighbors and relatives of how kind the LORD had been to her, and everyone rejoiced.

Luke 1:57-58, TLB

*"E*veryone rejoiced." Here in the beginning of the New Testament nestles a great story of God's power and people's pleasure; of God's kindness and people's joy; of God surmounting the impossible and a woman (past birthing age) delivering a boy. If you recall the beginning chapters of the Old Testament, there is a similar story of a very elderly couple (Abraham was 100; Sarah was 90) giving birth! But the hundreds of years between these two stories make no difference. God was still the God of the impossible—bringing joy to Elizabeth, laughter to Sarah, and both to those who shared their lives.

"Everyone rejoiced." Isn't it refreshing to think they took the time to do that? Zechariah and Elizabeth had waited so long—not just the normal nine months, but years—for a child. And neighbors, friends, and relatives did not let the event slip by unnoticed. Can you imagine the "oohs" and "aahs" as friends crowd into Elizabeth's house, peeking at the baby, giggling, jostling one another to see . . . leaving fruits, prepared breads, and a specially squeezed juice or two to refresh the new parents? How great their awe as Zechariah's voice (which God had removed for nine months) was restored to him, and they heard his exuberant, fresh praises to God. The surrounding hill country buzzed with excitement!

Yes, birth is indeed a time for great rejoicing! One of our friends recently gave birth. After the delivery, the husband filled the birthing room with streamers, banners, balloons, and exhilarating music. He brought in cake and punch, which he happily served to doctors, nurses, visitors, and hallway passersby. Everyone joined in the new parents' joy over the birth of their first-born!

Reflecting

1. What new joys and pleasures have you experienced since birthing?
2. What sentiments have your friends and relatives expressed regarding the birth? (List happy events, encouraging words, moments of awe and laughter, etc.)

Praying

Today, give special thanks (by name) to God for friends and relatives who have rejoiced with you. Pray for a specific blessing in their lives.

Unexpected Outcomes

*T*here was no happy laughter. They were stunned. How could this be? The pregnancy had gone so well. My friend had felt healthy. She had even eaten all the right foods! Nothing had prepared them for the baby that now lay in the bassinet with their name on it. Not long after birth she was diagnosed with Noonan syndrome, a congenital disease involving heart defects, cleft lip and palate (requiring tubal feedings into the stomach), developmental delay, hearing impairment in both ears, and a restricted airway.

Fears and questions chiseled away at what was to have been such a joyous celebration. Would she live or die? What would people think of her? Would she grow and develop? How could they possibly care for her? And why did *they* have an unhealthy child when the new parents peering with them through the nursery window had healthy ones?

But my friend and her husband took some positive steps forward. They allowed each other to express what they were thinking and feeling. They found that worry accomplishes nothing, while prayer accomplishes much. At times they would hold one another and "let the crying happen." They have stood face to face, encouraging one another through the grief and disappointment.

And they continued to accept the kindness of others; prepared meals, visits at the hospital during the ongoing multitude of treatments and operations, prayers and notes and calls of encouragement, and offers to babysit so the two of them could run errands or have a date night.

They have drawn closer to the God who formed this dear child in her mother's womb, and sense him much nearer. They have experienced again and again his understanding of their pain and demonstration of care for them.

Their special child has become a joy and delight as day by day they gain a deeper appreciation for life and for God because of her presence with them.

Reflecting

1. How is Jeremiah 1:5 a comforting Scripture to you? What does it tell us about God?
2. Has there been an inexplicable disappointment in your life? What positive steps forward have you taken?

Praying

Loving Creator, you make no mistakes. Help me to see every person as an intentional loving act on your part and treat them as such.

Faith in Difficult Circumstances

By faith Moses' parents hid him for three months after he was born, because they saw he was no ordinary child, and they were not afraid of the king's edict.

Hebrews 11:23

*F*rankly, we might say, how unwise, how unthinking, how inappropriate for Moses' parents to be pregnant. Talk about poor timing! They were slaves under a hostile government: If a boy were born, he would be killed. And how could they ever provide economically for a family? They already had two children, and humanly speaking, for these children a very bleak future lurked in the shadows of the Egyptian pyramids. And besides all that . . .

But wait! This wasn't just any old couple. These two people had *faith*—not an "I hope so, wringing-of-hands" sort of faith, but a "My-hope-rests-in-the-Almighty-God" kind of faith. *That* made all the difference in their world. They didn't know at that point that God had a plan for Moses to grow up in the palace as the son of Pharaoh's daughter, and then to be the one through whom God would lead his people out of the awful situation they were now in!

But with total trust in a living, powerful God, Moses' family moved into the first hours, days, and weeks of their baby's life, working together to protect and provide for this special child.

Reflecting

1. Has your faith been stretched with this birth? In what ways?
2. Was yours a planned pregnancy? If not, how have you been aware of the living God's help? And if so, what unplanned or unexpected events have taken place during these days, causing you to especially need God's help?

Praying

Loving God, thank you for the faith of Moses' parents, who believed that despite the difficult circumstances surrounding Moses' birth, God had a plan for this child's life. Help me to know that no matter what my plans or circumstances were or are, you have a very special plan for this child's life, and I can trust you to make it come about in your own time, in your own way.

The God of All Comfort

As a mother comforts her child, so will I comfort you.

Isaiah 66:13

"A flaw in *my* child?" Isn't that one of our greatest fears as a mom? It's almost impossible to bear *that* thought alongside the freshness, the beauty, the awesomeness and preciousness of this little one in our arms. And yet deep within ourselves, we know that is a possibility.

I arrived eight years after my second sister, unplanned, and another girl. Not only that, but I was also near death for the first three months of life because of a stricture in the esophagus. In the room adjoining the one in which Mother lay with me beside her, she overheard the doctor and nurse discussing my dilemma. "Well, we could operate," muttered the attending physician, "but probably she would not live through it."

My mother and dad returned home with no new baby in their arms. Years later, Mother still remembers the shock, the emptiness, the sense of loss and grief at not being able to nurse her new baby—and the fear of losing me forever. However, through the innovative intervention of a young female physician and the relentless nurturing of my mother, I was comforted, and I lived.

As you listen with new ears to your baby's slightest sounds of discomfort and immediately seek to alleviate the cause, remember: Your heavenly Father seeks to comfort you. As you feed your baby, remember: Your heavenly Father seeks to comfort you. As these first days and nights stretch you far beyond *your* comfort zone in comforting another, remember: God, with boundless energy, limitless compassion, endless wisdom, and unfathomable love, will comfort you "as a mother comforts her child." You and your heavenly Father have a *lot* in common—you both understand mothering.

And the "defect?" Well, *should* that appear in this child's life, in whatever form and at whatever time, you will be able, also, to embrace that as you keep knowing your loving God, the one who will comfort you "as a mother comforts her child."

Reflecting

1. What do you remember about *your* mother's ways of comforting you? What words and/or actions on her part bring a smile to your face as you reflect on this?
2. What comfort have you had from your heavenly Father during these weeks? Do you see any similarities between God's comforting and your mother's? What are they?

Praying

Dear Comforting God, I am so glad to know that you understand the complexities of mothering—the joys, the fears, the exasperations, and the deep satisfaction. Thank you, Lord, for comforting me even as I am trying to comfort my little one.

Multiple Births

My grace is sufficient for you, for my power is made perfect in weakness.

2 Corinthians 12:9

*F*lopsy, Mopsy, and Cottontail, the familiar threesome in *The Tale of Peter Rabbit,* intrigued me as a small child. Why? Well, in my picture book they look alike and are wearing identically colored cloaks. *Certainly,* deduced my wee mind, *they were born together. How wonderful to have several babies all at once and to be able to dress them just alike.* A romanticized view of multiple births? I'm afraid so. However, both my daughters experienced the same fantasy when they were young. "What fun to have twins and dress them alike," they dreamed aloud.

However, today's Scripture verse was emblazoned on my friend's mind when, in à nauseated daze, she heard the exuberantly reported results from her ultrasound: "You have twins!"

At that point in her life, she and her husband had a two-year-old, lived in an apartment, and drove a tiny car. She worked full-time at night to provide for their health insurance while her husband completed his degree.

Suddenly weakness permeated her life. Hospitalized for three months with preterm labor, she and her husband struggled to help their precious two-year-old understand the many changes. They bought a big car, moved to a new neighborhood and larger residence, and changed jobs—her husband to full-time work and she to the all-consuming activity of parenting *and* the ongoing adjustment of soon having three children who did not sleep for long periods. Lack of sleep has been perhaps the hardest of all adjustments. Finding anyone who could understand the depth of her fatigue was a challenge.

But as weakness penetrated, God's grace and power began to prevail! Through having her mom with her for an extended period of time, praying often, journaling the experience, talking with friends who had experienced multiple births, and accepting the help of others, my friend is embracing her new life with strength and renewed hope.

"Everything," she writes, "has changed in my life except God and my husband!"

Reflecting

1. If you have experienced multiple births, what strength, power, and grace have you found to help you through?
2. Whatever your circumstances upon entering motherhood, what fantasies about the role have you found untrue? How can you apply 2 Corinthians 12:9 to your life?

Praying

Loving Creator, thank you for helping me to deal with the realities of my life at this time. Please teach me how to apply your grace and power to my daily weaknesses.

Family Cooperation

And [Jochebed] became pregnant and gave birth to a son. When she saw that he was a fine child, she hid him for three months.

Exodus 2:2

As a new mom, this was one of the most astounding verses in the Bible to me!

Jochebed, an Israelite, and her family were slaves under Egyptian rule. At this particular time in history, every Israelite baby boy was to be killed because the Israelite male population was growing steadily and Egypt feared an insurrection. But lo and behold, Jochebed and her husband saved their baby's life and hid him for *three months!*

These people were not wealthy or even middle class. They did not live in a one-family dwelling, secluded from others by fences or rolling acres. They were slaves. Practically, this meant very close quarters with neighbors, paper-thin walls, and only one or, at most, two rooms for the entire family. Between the parents and Moses' two young siblings, the four of them didn't let him make a peep for ninety days! Just try to imagine the feeding, rocking, and other loving tactics employed to accomplish such a feat.

From a human perspective, keeping little Moses quiet for three months must have taken an awful lot of teamwork. Many times, as mothers, we can feel very lonely. We feel as though we are doing it all on our own. So much of what a very young baby needs right now, it needs from the mother. Sometimes this can cause the father to feel left out or neglected. It is important to remember, though, even at the very beginning, that parenting requires teamwork from start to finish.

And God works side by side with you, just as he worked alongside Moses' family throughout this harrowing experience. Baby Moses survived and grew to manhood, fulfilling the purpose God had for his life all along.

Reflecting

1. If you are with your spouse, is there an understanding of how to handle *together* the crying at night or fussing during daytime hours? What could you do together to improve support of one another during this time?
2. What changes is your family structure undergoing with the birth of your new one? How is God helping you to face those changes?

Praying

Loving God, I praise you that you are the God of the impossible, using what little we think we are and have to accomplish great and mighty feats for your glory. Thank you for this amazing story of baby Moses' family. Thank you for the protection, patience, and creativity you gave them. Thank you that you will continue to help my family, also, in the new changes taking place since the birth of our precious baby.

Finding Help

God is my helper. He is a friend of mine!

Psalm 54:4, *TLB*

*W*hen our first child was born, I was helped by my mother and relatives, plus a telephone at hand for an S.O.S. night or day. When our second child was born, a kind missionary co-worker reluctantly agreed to leave her husband and home, board an uncertain flight over the Peruvian Andes, and settle into our stark, nonapplianced adobe coastal house for two weeks. When number three appeared, no hope of help graced my doorway. In great desperation I succumbed to a cultural necessity—a live-in maid, someone I had never even seen before!

Throughout the whole time, from when I had my mother nearby, the closest woman in my life, to a time when help came from an absolute stranger four and a half years later, God kept letting me know that he was my helper and friend. Sometimes the packaging of that help was not what I expected. Yet each time that God-given post-delivery assistance began to recede so I could resume "normal" living, I experienced pangs of loss and anxiety. Would I be capable to face all the added demands this new little life had brought me?

Maybe you have similar thoughts today if your mother or someone dear has gone back home. Look around—you will find books, magazines, friends, church or club acquaintances, other family members . . . and through them all, "God is *your* helper. He is a friend of *yours.*" And he has someone—or some help nearby for you. Seek, and you will find who or what that is.

Reflecting

1. In what ways have you seen God's special help to you in the past two weeks?
2. How has he helped you unexpectedly?
3. Who or what has he brought to remind you that he is very aware of your needs?

Praying

Loving Creator, today I want to remind you *and* me that you are my helper and friend. Thank you for your help that has come in so many ways since the birth of my baby. Open my eyes to see what help is available to me today. And may I be grateful, no matter in what packaging that help may come.

Frustrations

Isaac pleaded with Jehovah to give Rebekah a child. . . . Then at last she became pregnant. And it seemed as though children were fighting each other inside her! "I can't endure this," she exclaimed. So she asked the Lord about it.

Genesis 25:21-22, TLB

*R*ebekah talked very openly with God. She wasted no time in going straight to him when she felt she'd had enough. Just one desperate sentence: "I can't endure this." Scripture doesn't tell us that God removed her discomfort, but if you read further along in that chapter, he *did* give her an answer.

Maybe your pregnancy was a breeze. Maybe you had great discomfort. Whichever the case, the baby is now in your arms at last. But today you may feel like Rebekah. There are some things about mothering, wifing, keeping the home, and just plain balancing life at this time that make you want to scream, "Help! I cannot endure this!"

Well, go ahead. Say that to the One who calls you by name, who is listening for your voice, and who will know exactly how to answer your exasperation.

Reflecting

1. Identify and write down in your journal what have been the hardest adjustments for you during the past two weeks. Talk to God about those things today.
2. Beside each adjustment that you wrote down, write the source of God's answer to you. Has it been prayer, a friend, a book or magazine, a song, or some other comfort? If the matter is still not solved, write down where you think you might be able to find help.

Praying

Comforting God, if not today, then someday soon, I'm sure I will feel just like Rebekah, shouting, "I cannot stand this!" Lord, thank you for allowing human feelings to be seen all over your written Word. I'm so glad my emotions are not a surprise or an offense to you. You made me, and I know you will help me. Thanks, Lord.

Gentleness

But we were gentle among you, like a mother caring for her little children.

1 Thessalonians 2:7

*I*n this surprising simile, Paul, the strong, vision-led, goal-driven missionary of first-century Christendom compares his treatment of others to that of a mother, gently caring for her little children. Gentleness—without harshness or violence. Gentleness—singular evidence that Jesus' Spirit is at home in us.

Once upon a time there was a set of grandparents. Their children had grown and moved on. They thought about their own deferred goals and happily pursued them.

Then someone knocked on the door. Their daughter, whose life was shaken, came with her baby and young child. They opened the door, providing a safe haven for the little family.

The grandmother worked. The grandfather worked. The daughter worked long and unusual hours. The grandfather told goodnight stories to the young child. The grandmother arose in the middle of the night to change the baby. The grandfather arose in the middle of the night to heat the bottle. The grandmother fed the baby. Later in the night the grandfather arose to give words of comfort to the young child. Later in the night the grandmother arose to give arms of comfort to the baby. The grandfather marveled at the gentleness of his wife with the baby.

The grandmother marveled at the gentleness of her husband with the young child.

Early each morning they awoke, bundled up the children, dropped them off at daycare before they entered their work, and picked them up at the end of the day.

The daughter spent all her spare time with her children. Though weary and worried, she read to them, played with them, helped them laugh, and prayed over them.

For the long months of renewed parenting, the grandparents gathered strength from God's gentleness with them. The daughter marveled at the gentleness of her parents. The parents marveled at the gentleness of their daughter. The little children breathed deeply from that gentleness. They lost their fears and snuggled close, growing within the singing voices of three adults, and were safe. Yes, gentleness begets gentleness, and the Lord God draws very near.

Reflecting

How has someone's gentleness encouraged you lately? Recall someone who was gentle with you as a child. How did that make you feel?

Praying

Loving God, I thank you today for those I remember who were gentle with me when I was small. Give me your gentleness today with all small children.

Facing Reality: Weariness

*I lift up my eyes
to the
hills—where
does my help
come from? My
help comes from
the LORD, the
Maker of heaven
and earth. He
will not let your
foot slip—he
who watches
over you will not
slumber.*

Psalm 121:1-3

*T*oday you may be in circumstances you are not shouting over with delight! The writer of the above words hit on a life truth. Our basic strength, help, or encouragement cannot always come from our circumstances or physical surroundings—whether they are the Colorado mountains, the Illinois prairies, or the North Dakota plains. Rather, our inner strength and help *can* come directly from the very One who made all of these!

Amazingly, God, the maker of heaven and earth, is keenly aware of the movement of your feet, where you go, and how slowly or unsurely you move. As you scuff along to the bathroom, the bedroom, or the kitchen, and then retrace those steps (how many times in a day or night?), he is watching. As you tuck those feet up to rest, or move them gently to the rhythm of a rocking chair while cuddling your newborn, he is watching over you.

And he never goes to sleep. When you are bending over this soft little bundle in the night to lift her, comfort her, diaper her, or feed her, remember that your heavenly Father is bending over you. You are not alone. He will strengthen you. He will sustain you. *You* are *his* primary care. And he knows that you are not God! You *do* need to sleep.

With our first child, that first night home from the hospital was a living nightmare for me. If she snuffled, I flew to the bassinet. If she was quiet, I also flew to her side, certain that I had somehow smothered her. Oh, that I had listened to a loving husband's advice (I wrongly thought him quite callous at the time!) and remembered that we had done our best, I needed to sleep, and God was wide awake, watching over us all!

Reflecting

1. What "ideal" circumstance, surroundings, and support have you had to let go of in these first days of mothering?
2. Focus on someone or something within your setting that can remind you that *God* is your helper, no matter what the geographical or physical circumstances are. Who or what may that be?

Praying

Loving Creator, thank you that you never sleep. You consider me such a treasure that you never take your eyes off me. So help me, Lord, to close my eyes and rest, knowing that you will care for what I, a frail human, cannot.

Our Mothering God

Can a mother forget the baby at her breast and have no compassion on the child she has borne? Though she may forget, I will not forget you! See, I have engraved you on the palms of my hands.

Isaiah 49:15-16

What an absurd question God poses! I thought in my youth. In my naivete, I wondered *what* mother would or possibly ever *could* forget the baby she is nursing or have no compassion, no compelling kind actions, toward the child she labored so hard and long to bring to birth. But we need only pause, read, listen, watch . . . and yes, horrifyingly enough, there are indeed mothers in the world, in our own country, in our own cities, like the one God describes.

History proves that there have always been mothers who for ungodly motives (be it an extramarital affair, reckless pursuit of money, or cultural pressures) abandoned the one who once nestled safely within their womb. Perhaps that's why Paul had to remind Christians in Titus 2:4 that older women need to *teach* younger women to love their children.

Our God thoroughly understands mothers and mothering. He understands the worry and fear, the restlessness and impatience, the tiredness and crankiness that can creep up on a mom and incapacitate her in her tracks! For that reason, he stands beside you today to mother you. In this beautiful analogy, the greatest parent of all, God, declares that although a human mother may do the unnatural and forget her child, he will *never, never* forget you. It is as if your name were tatooed on his palms. So when-ever he holds up his hands, he sees your name and is reminded of you—you, his very own child.

Reflecting

1. Although you may normally think of God as Father, what new perspective do you gain about him when you consider this image of God as mother?
2. How and when have you experienced this kind of maternal care from God?

Praying

Dear loving God, I am in awe today of your being not only a father to me but also a mother. Thank you for this beautiful imagery that reminds me that my name is always before you and you will never forget me. Keep teaching me to love this precious child, even as you love me.

New Birth

Jesus replied, "With all the earnestness I possess I tell you this: Unless you are born again, you can never get into the Kingdom of God."

John 3:3, TLB

Birth . . . perhaps the most important event in your life, since it allowed you to experience existence in this world; and so *birth*days have been happily celebrated since ancient times. In many countries the very first birthday is celebrated extradordinarily because the baby has survived disease, hunger, and adverse climate conditions.

Rebirth . . . and I can hear you saying, "Wait, let's not talk about that. It's too close to what I just went through in giving birth!" But this isn't about going back into a *womb*—but rather about coming out of a *tomb!* Because God says we're *dead* without Jesus Christ in our lives. It's only by being born again, rebirthed, restored to friendship with God, our Creator, in whose image we are made, that real life becomes ours. How? By simply praying: "God, I know I am a sinner. I believe in Jesus Christ, your Son, who died on the cross in my place, for my sins. Please forgive me, come into my life, and take complete control." And he will!

This is what Jesus meant by "You must be born again." His Spirit will enter your life, and you will experience forgiveness, peace, and guidance like you never knew was possible. What an amazing moment it was in your life journey when you physically birthed a new life! Are you willing to let God spiritually birth new life within you?

As you enjoy the precious new life you hold in your arms, rejoice in the new life God offers you within!

Reflecting

1. Where are you right now in the spiritual birthing process? Not yet in process? Recently birthed? Strong and growing?
2. What steps do you need to take to be where you would like to be spiritually? Think of someone you can share your thoughts with or ask questions. Plan to do so in the next two days.

Praying

Loving Creator, I thank you that you not only care about physical life, but you are concerned about restoring me spiritually. I accept today anew your free gift of salvation and praise you for your freeing, empowering presence in my life.

Adoption

As the focus of his love, long, long ago [God] decided to adopt us into his family through Jesus Christ.

Ephesians 1:4-5, The Message

*L*ove—it can certainly propel you into uncharted waters!

For instance, take my friend and her husband—feeling whole and content with their two teenage sons. Then in a meeting one afternoon they heard of unborn twin girls who would need a home. Without prior consultation, they both shot up a hand simultaneously, saying, "We can do that," then stared at each other in shocked amazement!

And so it came to be. It was certainly not an easy process. It was a very arduous one, with many moments of anguish, doubt, and stress.

All of us who decide to parent take a risk. We cannot ensure the outcome, neither for ourselves nor for the child. But I've always admired those who adopt—those like my friend, who open their arms because of a baby's great need. Not because it's an especially comfortable step for them to take or because they have lots of time, money, and energy, but because of *love*.

For instance, take God. Even before the "in the beginning" of Genesis 1, God had thought about you and me. Aware already of our great need, he focused his love on us and put in motion a plan to adopt us as his very own to be co-heirs with his son, Jesus Christ. And my friend tells me that the adopted child can never be disinherited—never written off. Legally, that child has the same right as the birthed child.

Just think—God, in his great mercy, adopted us into a new family relationship of trust and love and an immense inheritance—eternal life—which we cannot begin to imagine! And while we're still here, he has placed within us his Holy Spirit, who affirms that we are truly children of God.

Was the process of our adoption easy for God? Hardly. It cost him the life of his only Son, Jesus Christ. Because of love, *God's* unfathomable love, you and I can experience today the grace-filled, far-reaching effects of adoption in our own lives.

Reflecting

1. What are your feelings toward God as you consider what it cost him to adopt you?
2. If you have a friend who has adopted a child, encourage her today—tell her how proud you are of her.

Praying

Loving God, how grateful I am for your love to me, long before I ever even thought about you. Thank you for adopting me into your family. Please give me encouraging and kind words for those who have reached out and adopted a child.

Wakeful Nights

On my bed I remember you; I think of you through the watches of the night. Because you are my help, I sing in the shadow of your wings. My soul clings to you; your right hand upholds me.

Psalm 63:6-8

*T*he psalmist David was spending many wakeful nights when he wrote these words to God. Wakeful nights, not because of a new baby, but because he was hiding out in desert caves, still running from King Saul.

By now, you may be getting a little weary of your baby's crying at night. Be comforted to know that a lot of us grandmothers empathize with you. We remember well those nights—with *you* in our arms!

The amazing thing about David is that in his discomfort and confusion, he didn't forget who had the answers and who could help him. This situation for him lasted at least seven years. Your situation, God willing, will last only a few weeks, and at most, a few months. Do not despair. Remember that your whole being (physical, emotional, mental, and spiritual) has undergone tremendous changes, and that phasing into motherhood is still a process for you. Give yourself (and encourage others to give you) time and space to absorb it all.

Reflecting

1. What positive actions did David take in his nighttime wakefulness?
2. Do you feel upheld by your God? Why or why not? If not, what might increase your sense of being upheld by him?
3. Take some time today to *remember* God, to *sing,* and *cling* to him and his promises.

Praying

Dear Comforter, you know how many new things I have stuffed into my mind during these days . . . from schedules to formulas and sleepless nights to daily hours alone with the baby. But help me, above all, to remember you and remember that you are always here with me. I am very grateful for that.

Team Parenting

*An angel of the
Lord appeared
to him in a
dream and said,
"Joseph son of
David, do not be
afraid to take
Mary home as
your wife,
because what is
conceived in her
is from the Holy
Spirit."*

Matthew 1:20

*T*eamwork in parenting—has any couple on earth ever lived this more deeply than Mary and Joseph, birthing and rearing the Son of God? Teamwork—not just two listening to one another but rather *three:* God, Mary, and Joseph, with the latter two listening to God.

We know that both Mary and Joseph were good, upright, God-fearing people. But for a moment, put yourself in their sandals. Consider the magnitude of their commitment to God, to one another, and to the Child. This commitment involved:

Life-changing decisions—to believe God in the face of public disgrace and disbelief, to follow the directions of angels, and to move the whole family at least three times, once in the middle of the night to a foreign country to escape death. To whom could they explain these strange actions? What intimate friends Mary and Joseph had to become as they were bound together by God through unusual beginnings and unusual risks.

Life-altering disciplines—to *not* consummate the marriage until *after* Jesus' birth. For months this couple, with all the new-lywed passion and desire for one another, waited until after the birth of the Child. Sustained by God they waited, in spite of the natural aching for one another. However they experienced some measure of release, it did not come from their coupling with each other or with another outside of the marriage. They stood firmly together, through an unusual period of life, to be participants in a singular miracle.

Life-preserving foundations—to center their parenting around the Word of God, to worship together with other people of faith, and to commit themselves to the home and to faithful provision for their family. They did not hide from family, society, or the congregation because they were parenting an unusual child. In fact, God eventually brought them back to Nazareth, where the rumors as well as the miracle had begun. Through the years, eyebrows were raised and questions were asked to which Mary and Joseph could not respond. They stood together, committing their cause to the God who had called them on this journey. What a model team!

Reflecting

What impresses you about the teamwork of Mary and Joseph? What would you like to bring into your parenting from this story?

Praying

Loving God, I am overwhelmed by Mary and Joseph's commitment to you and your will. Teach me what you want me to learn from this beautiful, godly team.

God as Parent

*W*hat an excellent parent is God our Father. In this short quote (which the prophet Isaiah communicated to the Israelites during one of their often-needed reassurance periods), God himself practices three good parenting habits: touch, conversation, and presence. He assured the Israelites and assures us today that he is "holding us by our right hand"—he is touching us. How often we are energized by the kind touch of someone near us.

God also said, "I say to you, . . ." He communicated with them, letting them know that he understood their feelings: "Don't be afraid." Isn't it great to converse with someone who understands our feelings?

And then our heavenly Father said, "I am here to help you." The leader Moses at one point told God he would go any-where—*if* God's presence would go with him. And Jesus reit-erated that concept in the New Testament, saying that he would never leave us nor abandon us.

Touch energizes us, conversation stimulates us, and presence reassures us. You are probably becoming a pro with your baby in these three areas. How much she wants (and cries for!) your presence, your touch, and your conversation. More and more she will focus on your face—the most beloved face to her on the earth.

Just have fun today enjoying the beginning responses of your little one to these three actions on your part!

Reflecting

1. In your journal, write down one instance of:
   —how you have sensed God's touch on your life
   —how God has communicated with you
   —how you have sensed God's presence
2. What do you feel when your baby responds to your presence, voice, and touch? Why do you think our heavenly Father says we must come to him with a childlike heart and attitude?
3. Who in your life at this time has energized and encouraged you through their touch, their presence, or their words?

Praying

Thank God for what you jotted down in question 1. Thank him also for those people you listed in question 3.

The God Who Is There

By day the LORD went ahead of them in a pillar of cloud to guide them on their way and by night in a pillar of fire to give them light, so that they could travel by day or night.

Exodus 13:21

*H*ave you ever wished for such explicit and visible direction from God as the Israelites had as they fled the slavery of Egypt? God was never out of their sight, either by day or by night. By day the cloud showed them the way through an all-new terrain, and in the heavy blackness of a desert night, an ever-present glow from the pillar of light seeped through the thickest tent dwelling. God was near; his people knew he was present.

But think of what led up to that freedom march. Imagine it from the perspective of a pregnant woman or a new mom with an infant in her arms.

Think of the intense preparations for the trip and the questions that would fill your mind as you work—What about food supplies, shelter, danger, wild animals, and care for your new baby? Or if you are pregnant, where would you be when you delivered? Are you strong enough for the journey? Do Moses and God really know what they're doing?

Hours later, you are scurrying with the multitudes through an immense tunnel of water walls. Safe, finally, on the opposite side of the Red Sea, you watch with open-mouthed relief as those same walls come crashing down on your Egyptian pursuers. With the other Israelite women, you rummage around in your cloth bag to find your tambourine. Following Miriam, Moses' sister, you dance to her victory-filled chant.

It doesn't take too many miles for you to realize, though, that some things never change—even on a God-given, God-driven journey such as this one. People complain about lacks: lack of food, water, comforts—anything slightly positive they can remember about those "good ol' Egyptian days." It is hard not to join in. But manna falls from heaven to feed you and your traveling companions. It's always there and in sufficient supply, just as God promised. You also begin to notice that your clothes never wear out. Good thing! There isn't the slightest *mirage* of a mall up ahead!

And one more thing that especially the women comment on is that no one's feet swell, *ever:* not in all the walking, standing, hot weather, not even in pregnancy! Yes, God is near; God is present.

Reflecting

Compared with your Israelite sister, what do you have to be grateful for? What do you want to learn from her?

Praying

Dear God, help me to see you in my present situation and be thankful.

The God Who Sees and Hears

*W*ho was this person to whom "the angel of the Lord" (considered an appearance of the preincarnate Christ) appeared for the *first* time in the beginning pages of the Bible? An Old Testament patriarch? A well-known woman of faith? An aged, faithful follower of God? None of the three.

The person was Hagar, a young slave girl from Egypt, given as a gift to Abraham as he and his wife, Sarah, traveled through that region. When the angel of the Lord appeared to Hagar, she was pregnant by Abraham (through the desire of Sarah, her mistress, and according to cultural customs) and running away from the jealous rage of this same woman. Thrust out into the desert to die—by a foreigner who hated her, from a career track she had not chosen, because of a plot she did not devise—she was found by God.

He found her, collapsed, in the hot, arid desert, by a spring. God's words and actions toward this young, unwanted, unknown, unloved woman ring with hope for us today. We also may feel unwanted, unknown, unloved—or we may know someone else who feels that way. Yet here, among the first stories of the Bible, God's concern for the well-being of a pregnant woman and her unborn child draws us to him.

God let Hagar know that he *saw* and *heard* her. He said, "I have heard of your misery." And he even gave her the promise that she would indeed bear a son and should name him *Ishmael,* meaning "God hears." She, in awe, gave God the name *El-Shaddai,* meaning "You are the God who sees me." This most personal You-See-Me-God also dialogued with Hagar. He asked her two questions: "Where have you come from?" and "Where are you going?"

The outcome of that amazing encounter was that Hagar, the unknown, the unwanted, the unloved, went back to live in the tent of her mistress as Hagar the known, the wanted, the loved, empowered by God's presence and promises. She gave birth to a son, and Abraham named him Ishmael: "God hears."

Reflecting

As you consider Hagar's story, can you identify with her in trying to run away from a problem, being unhappy in a relationship, or facing circumstances out of your control? Whatever your circumstances, how do you know God sees and hears you?

Praying

Loving God, I pray for those women who are in circumstances they have not chosen. Please give them help and hope, as you did to Hagar.

Jesus' Happy Invitation

*Then she went
her way and ate
something, and
her face was
no longer
downcast. . . .
Then Hannah
prayed and said:
"My heart
rejoices in the
LORD."*

1 Samuel 1:18 and 2:1

Hannah, confined by her Maker,
 provoked by her adversary,
 misunderstood by husband and priest,
 she stood, and while the priest sat . . .

Hannah, weeping,
 bitterly weeping in grief,
 in anguish,
 weeping her soul inside-out
 until *all* (grief, anguish, bitterness)
 all is poured out in *petition*
 before the throne of her Maker.
 . . . and the priest began to understand and offer blessing.

Hannah, quiet and at peace . . .
 worshipping and praising God . . .

Hannah, cradling at her breast the fruit of her petition.

And what is the anguish in your soul? What is the grief in mine?

"Until now," says Jesus, "you have not asked for anything in my name. *Ask* and *you will receive,* and your joy, well, your joy will be a river overflowing its banks!" (See John 16:24)

Reflecting

1. What have you asked and received from God recently that gives you great joy?
2. With such an enthusiastic invitation from Jesus himself to ask so that we may have complete joy, write below what you will ask today. And then, ask.

Praying

Jesus, thank you for so strongly and clearly commanding me to lay out my petitions before you. You teach me that I am not to harbor hurt, misunderstanding, or fear within me, but I am to ask you for whatever I need, whether it is so small or so large in my eyes. Thank you that your desire is to see me full of believing joy today.

The God Who Answers Prayer

"I am the woman who stood here that time praying to the Lord. I asked him to give me this child, and he has given me my request; and now I am giving him to the Lord for as long as he lives." So she left [the child] there . . . for the Lord to use.

1 Samuel 1:27, TLB

*W*hat a beautiful portrait of the decisive woman Hannah: a woman who said what she meant and meant what she said!

She had waited a long time for this beloved child, Samuel. And the waiting was enveloped in suffering because Elkanah, her husband, had a second wife. Peninnah had children and delighted in provoking and irritating Hannah with these God-given gifts.

It was hard for Hannah's loving husband to understand her emptiness as he saw her tears, listless eating patterns, and despondency. In his bewilderment and naiveté (since he had the satisfaction of parenting children through another woman) he once asked her, "Don't I mean more to you than ten sons?" The answer, unrecorded, was obvious.

And then one day Hannah acted. She pulled herself together, walked into the temple, and "poured out her soul to the Lord." All her frustration and heartache welled up in spoken words to her Creator God. Weeping, she told God that if he would give her a son, she would give the son back to him, to serve him all the days of his life.

Eli, the priest, misunderstood Hannah as she wept and prayed inaudibly, thinking she was drunk. But when she explained that her prayer came from deep anguish and grief, Eli blessed her, asking the Lord to grant her petition, whatever it was. God gave Hannah her heart's desire—a son. And lo and behold, Hannah kept *her* promise!

When Samuel was weaned, perhaps at about three years of age, she took him to the temple and deposited him in Eli's care. And there Samuel lived and grew, later becoming the most revered priest the nation of Israel ever had.

Was that the extent of God's answer to Hannah's prayer? No. In 1 Samuel 2 we're told that "the Lord was gracious to Hannah; she conceived and gave birth to three sons and two daughters."

Reflecting

1. What in this vignette of Hannah makes you admire her?
2. What do you think it cost Hannah to act, instead of continuing her pattern of weeping and despair?
3. What part of this story do you sense the Spirit of God is applying to you? How will you respond?

Praying

Dear Creator God, Thank you for the decisiveness of Hannah, who came to you in faith. Help me today to not complain, but to live intentionally and truthfully before you and others.

Guardian Angels

See that you do not look down on one of these little ones. For I tell you that their angels in heaven always see the face of my Father in heaven.

Matthew 18:10

*G*loriously radiant, powerful beyond science fiction imagination, organized in ranks moving at God's command, angels are mentioned close to three hundred times in the Bible. And although they fight cosmic battles, contending against evil forces for nations, they also concern themselves for us individually, perhaps their greatest personal concern being for those who are weakest and most vulnerable—children.

In Scripture, at least two babies were protected through the overt intervention of these magnificent beings.

Genesis, first book of the Old Testament, records the story of Ishmael, still in the womb of his young mother, Hagar, abandoned to die in the desert. The angel of the Lord appeared, giving a promise of hope to Hagar, guiding her back to her mistress. Baby Ishmael, within the womb, escaped the desert doom of his depressed mother, later becoming the father of many nations.

Matthew, first book of the New Testament, records the story of Jesus, the Son of God. King Herod was intent on killing this unique child. Again it was an angel who frustrated that sinister plan. He appeared to Joseph in a dream, warning him to flee with his family to Egypt. Baby Jesus escaped the savage sword of a demented tyrant and became the Savior of all nations.

What consolation! In the midst of a mind-boggling diversity of duties—from unceasing worship of God in the heavenlies to treacherous wars with evil forces throughout the universe—babies, "little ones," hold preeminence on the list of angels' priorities.

The same angel that looks after your child has instantaneous audience with the King of kings. No boggled telephone lines. No impersonal voicemail system. Rather, ongoing face-to-face dialogue with the One who created your little one. Wouldn't you love to hear the conversation between your baby's angel(s) and God? What is asked? What is reported? What is treasured in the heavenlies about your sweet child?

Reflecting

1. What are some of the ways we can look down on a little child?
2. What practical steps can we take to avoid demeaning children?

Praying

Loving God, I thank you for your legions of angels, caring for our children and interacting with you about them. Please enable me to be intentional in lifting up these little ones to you and building them up with help, hope, and happiness in their growing process.

Ministering Angels

*O*ne of our little ones grew into a young woman. On a sunny spring day she waited alone at a street corner for the city bus to take her to high school.

A low-slung sedan cruised by. She paid little attention as she shifted her heavy bookbag to the other shoulder. A few minutes later the car returned more slowly. This time two men rolled down their windows, whistling and making lewd remarks. She stepped quickly away from the corner, wishing desperately for the bus. Her mouth was dry. She prayed. Her heart pounded. An oppressive, sickening *aloneness* swept over her in the middle of this bright day, in the middle of this bustling city.

The car slammed to a stop beside her. She froze. A man jumped out, cursing and muttering, "Baby, we're really gonna make you work now!" Roughly propelled toward the open car door, she moved as if she were in a trance.

Suddenly loud screams pierced the ominous afternoon silence. Strong hands tore her free from the man's crunching grip. Doors banged shut as the car sped out of sight.

Our daughter stood speechless, shaking. On either side of her stood a punk-rocker, holding her up, protecting her. Two young men who three minutes before were nowhere in sight.

Are not all angels ministering spirits sent to serve those who will inherit salvation?

Hebrews 1:14

Two young men she did not know, nor had she ever seen. Two young men who calmed her and insisted on accompanying her.

They did. They waited in silence. They boarded the bus and sat with her. They delivered her inside the front door of the school. And then—they were gone. Gone were the ones sent to protect our child. Gone . . . but not far away.

I believe in angels.

Reflecting

In your journal, write your response to the truth of protective angels around your child throughout his or her life.

Praying

Holy God, I thank you that unseen angels are aware of my child and his needs, not only today, but throughout his life. That is a great comfort to me, and I praise you.

Overcoming Fears

In Luke 1:29-30, The Living Bible uses three words to describe Mary's reaction to the Angel Gabriel's alarming appearance: *confused, disturbed,* and *frightened.* Any wonder?! Mary was a young, modest woman, quietly, happily engaged to an upright man, preparing for the soon-coming celebration of their union. Everything was marching in normal, Jewish-ordered custom. Then suddenly, without warning, a shimmering, gigantic God-sent messenger, Gabriel himself, appeared! How would you have reacted?

So what transpired between Mary's first reaction and the response to her cousin Elizabeth a few days later, recorded in today's Scripture? Mary heard the angel's pronouncement: She would conceive, the baby would be a boy, he would be very great, he would be called the Son of God, he would occupy the throne of David, reigning over Israel forever, and his kingdom would never end. Gabriel then tied a big bow on this mind-boggling package: "For every promise from God shall surely come true." And Mary (how did she find her voice?) verbally affirmed this momentous, unexpected work of God in her life: "May everything you said come true."

Mary responded, "Oh, how I praise the Lord. How I rejoice in God my Savior!"

Luke 1:46-47, TLB

What had transpired in Mary? Her focus had changed from *how* this would come about to *who* was in control. And in that moment she believed that what God said, he would accomplish. So that a portion of Elizabeth's prophetic greeting to Mary was "You believed that God would do what he said; that is why he has given you this wonderful blessing." Faith in the faithful God turned Mary's confusion and fear into a song of praise and joy!

Reflecting

1. What are some of the fears in your life that can be overcome when you focus on what God can and will do to fulfill his promises?
2. What can you let go of today, rolling it onto God's shoulders so that Luke 1:46-47 can be your response and motivate your actions?
3. What promise from Scripture will help to remind you today of God's faithfulness?

Praying

Loving God, help me today to emulate Mary's example of faith-filled actions and belief in your promises, even though I cannot see the future. Help me to act out of faith today and not from fear.

Fear and Creativity

*R*emember the story of David and King Saul? David the thoughtful musician, Saul the jealous politician; David running, Saul pursuing; David hiding, Saul seeking. When David composed these words of praise to God, he had just come through one of his most frightening experiences. Fleeing Saul, David headed for help to the supposedly friendly king of Gath. When he arrived, however, he found that his fame had preceded him and death awaited there, too. He escaped by feigning insanity.

Fear is a paralyzer of life, joy, and all creativity. It makes us feel like a situation is impossible and we are incompetent to face it.

In today's Scripture, David said that he sought God and God delivered him from all his fears. Is it possible, then, that this loving God, upon delivering David from fear, gave him the creative idea to act insane and thereby escape?

Raising three small children, far from any ongoing stimulus for my musical abilities, I feared I would never again play the piano as once I had. I believed that so resolutely that it became a stalking fear in my life. However, through prayer and the positive, practical encouragement of my husband (who spent hours watching the children while I practiced!) I returned once again to perform a concerto with a renowned pianist in our coastal Peruvian city!

Perhaps today you are struggling with a fear related to your new baby. Rather than letting that fear paralyze you and zap your joy, try what David did. Name the fear aloud to God, verbally hand it over to him, and wait expectantly for God to give you a creative way to meet the challenge.

Reflecting

1. Think of a fear you had recently. How did God deliver you from that fear? As you reflect, did God provide some creative way for you to move ahead with confidence?
2. Is there some fear invading your thinking today? According to Psalm 34, what can you do to be released from that?
3. In your journal today, write down some words of praise to the Lord. How can you "boast in the Lord"? Who can you call to glorify the Lord with you today?

Praying

Dear Comforter, if fears invade my mind today, help me to seek you, remembering that you will deliver me from those fears. Thank you for doing so in the past. Thank you for friends with whom I can talk about how wonderful you are to me, and friends with whom I can pray.

Faith and Parenting

*[Jesus said,]
"Everything is
possible for him
who believes."
Immediately the
boy's father
exclaimed, "I do
believe; help me
overcome my
unbelief!"*

Mark 9:23-24

*E*ach of the four Gospels gives descriptive accounts of Jesus being there for parents and their children. Some children were sick, some were dying, others were even dead—but Jesus brought them back to life! To the many incidents of parents and children (some children with needy parents and some parents with needy children), Jesus responded personally with care and perception.

I identify with this story in Mark, because this father confesses having a mixed bag in the area of faith, as I often have. He admits that he has some unbelief as well. Jesus gives the man the opportunity to tell the truth about his doubts. When the father responds truthfully, Jesus makes the "everything is possible" *real* in his life. The son is healed.

Not every sick child is accounted for in the short Gospel narratives. Certainly not all were healed, any more than all the sick adults in Israel were made well during Jesus' earthly stay. But God *was* present, understanding and embracing the pain that parents experience with their children, understanding the human frailty of teetering between faith and unbelief.

There are three beautiful facets to this story: the miracle of the boy's healing, the honest disclosure of the father's struggle, and the compassion of God's work through it all. Jesus said, "Everything is possible for him who believes." The "everything is possible" does not always mean the outcome that we want (such as total healing). It may mean that he will enable us to have great patience. It may mean that his glory will be seen in unbelievable ways in our life as we go through difficult circumstances. What it *does* mean is that when we draw close to God in honesty, with the faith we have, he enables us to accept his will in our path of parenting.

Reflecting

1. Based on Jesus' response to this man's honesty, how do you think God views the pockets of unbelief in the fabric of our life?
2. What about Jesus' attitude encourages you to confide in him with *your* needs?

Praying

Jesus, I want to be much more honest with you in prayer. From this story in the Scriptures, I know I *can* be honest with you. I can admit areas of unbelief and ask for your help in overcoming them. May my child grow up mimicking my openness with you.

Worrying

Look at the birds of the air; they do not sow or reap or store away in barns, and yet your heavenly Father feeds them. Are you not much more valuable than they? Who of you by worrying can add a single hour to your life?

Matthew 6:26-27

*Y*es, step outside. Look up. Observe the birds.

On a quiet summer morning I told a friend good-bye at the door of her house. Suddenly she reached out. "Come," she insisted, taking me by the arm, "You have to see something." Guiding me under the multiple trees in her yard, she directed, "Look up."

At first I couldn't see them. The camouflage of layered leaves and dark bark was perfect. My eyes probed beyond the general beauty to exact detail. Yes, there they were. Two baby robins, heads thrown back, eyes closed, mouths open in expectation, in complete trust, in a "do or die" mode. Obviously they were not worried. Obviously they knew their open mouths would be rewarded with sustenance. Obviously they had parents who were off on a quick trip to the supermarket.

Yet Jesus didn't say, "Look at the birds. Their parents feed them." He said, "Look at the birds. *Your heavenly Father* feeds them."

Though God truly cares for the birds and is aware when even the smallest plummets to the ground, Jesus' question in today's Scripture intimates that *you and your child* are of much more value to him than the birds.

So lean back, open your spiritual eyes, ears, and mouth, and let God feed you. Maybe the food will come through a song or a friend's encouraging phone call, a word from the Bible, or a positive thought given by the Holy Spirit. As you are fed by God today, you'll find the worries being replaced by faith in an ever-present God, the God who whispers, "Step outside. Look up. Observe the birds. Are you not much more valuable than they?"

Reflecting

1. What is one way within your daily routine that you make time to let God feed you?
2. Tonight write down one concern, one worry that was turned to trust in God through the day.

Praying

Loving God, thank you for the living examples you have placed around me that reflect your care of your creatures, and especially of the children you created. Give me the faith of newborn birds, knowing you will sustain me as I reach out to sustain this new life you have given me.

Believing for Another

Then little children were brought to Jesus for him to place his hands on them and pray for them.

Matthew 19:13

*H*ow would the little children have gotten to Jesus if no one had brought them? How would they have experienced Jesus unless someone believed he could help them?

Again and again in the New Testament, we find people bringing children with needs to Jesus.

When Jesus freed the boy from demon-prompted seizures, it was because the father asked for Jesus' help.

When Jesus healed the Canaanite woman's little girl, it was because the mother asked for Jesus' help.

When Jesus gave back life to a young girl who had died, it was because the father asked for Jesus' help.

Bringing and *believing*. The ones in need did not have the capacity for either bringing themselves to Jesus or believing in him. Those who loved them brought them and believed for them.

As a new mom, you have the unique opportunity and privilege to bring your little child and her needs before a listening, loving God—a good God who will respond to your faith.

Use your *bring-believe privilege* often. God *will* bless your child, and you will be refreshed and restored in the ripples of that blessing.

Reflecting

1. Imagine yourself in the New Testament setting. Place your baby in Jesus' hands. Hear him pray for your child. How do you feel? How do you respond?
2. What time of the day (or night) could you daily bring your child to God in prayer? What is a specific need that your child has today?

Praying

Dear God, thank you for the privilege I have of bringing my baby's needs to you and believing for her. Thank you for responding to her needs because of my faith.

Woman-to-Woman Encouragement

At the angel Gabriel's appearance to Mary, God gave these very sensitive and sensible words to a young teenager now pregnant with God's will: "Even Elizabeth your relative is going to have a child in her old age, and she who was said to be barren is in her sixth month. Nothing is impossible with God."

Certainly both God *and* Mary realized that this divine plan would cause suffering for her, Joseph, and their families. God did not overlook Mary's humanness or her innate need for space and sharing with another woman. The angel Gabriel became God's "telephone line" to Mary with the astounding news of his miraculous work in another woman's life—and a relative and friend, at that! Mary picked up on God's suggestion for her encouragement. She packed her bags immediately!

Perhaps it was on that long, four-day walk to a Judean village in the hill country that Mary reflected on the story of Hannah from the Old Testament, which then became the background for her own inspired song in Luke 2. But surely in all of her ponderings she could not have envisioned the greeting that awaited her as Elizabeth threw open the door in welcome. And *most* surely, neither had Elizabeth planned for the joyous leap within her womb nor the prophetic words that spilled exuberantly from her lips, blessing this young woman, acknowledging that the one in Mary's womb was greater than the child in her own, and confirming that what the angel had proclaimed *would indeed* take place.

How kind of God to orchestrate that woman-to-woman encounter. And what humility in Elizabeth to not have any jealousy toward Mary. She, the older woman, the recipient of such a singular blessing from the Lord, did not try to upstage Mary, but in genuine humility recognized the superior blessing God had given her young cousin. Wouldn't you love to have heard their conversations and prayers for the next three months?

Reflecting

1. Name the people who were your support system during your pregnancy. Recall God's kindness in bringing them across your path.
2. What impresses you most about this whole story of God, the angel Gabriel, the Holy Spirit, Elizabeth, and Mary?

Praying

Dear Comforter, today I give thanks to you for those you placed around me during the months of pregnancy—for their kind words and actions. And I also thank you for the example of Mary and Elizabeth: Mary, willing to say yes to you no matter the cost, and Elizabeth, willing to allow your Spirit to work in her for the blessing of another. May I follow in their footsteps.

Loving Your Child

Then [older, mature women] can train the younger women to love their husbands and children.

Titus 2:4

*B*efore I married, I thought it odd that this verse seemed to imply that young women needed to be trained to love their children. Weren't all little children wonderful? And didn't every mom have that innate love and patience for her own child? *First-century women must have been really strange,* I concluded.

Then I overheard a respected young mom recount to my mother how there were days when she cried out to the Lord for love in dealing with her three little boys, born within four years.

Later, in the second month of my first pregnancy, a woman in Christian service told me that she had been a "very spiritual person" until her children came along, but that now patience with her children was impossible—evidenced by her continual screaming at them and at everyone else. She assured me that I would be the same—"just wait and see!"

But it wasn't until my own children began to appear that the wisdom of this verse made sense to me. Yes, as a new mom I needed the training and encouragement, by word and by example, of mature women.

And God brought that, even though the help came through a male author and three women who were not mothers! One was married without children, and two were single and of a different nationality. The verse doesn't say that they have to be *mothers*. It says *mature*. For two of my friends, their maturity came from teaching the Bible and from having observed a lot of child-rearing—positive and negative! The third young woman empathized with me and with the *children!* But all three women gave me laughter, creative help, and childcare at different points in the midst of day-in, day-out life with three little people.

Once again I recognize that God, from the beginning, has understood all the phases of a woman's life and in great love and wisdom has mapped out the support system: woman to woman—whether mother, daughter, sister, aunt, niece, grandmother, co-worker, or Christian sister. Right now, there's a woman near you who understands and can help you. . . .

Reflecting

1. What older woman's life or words have encouraged you so far in your mothering?
2. Make the time to call her or drop her a note of thanks.

Praying

Creator God, thank you for understanding my needs as a mom and for placing women around me. Help me to be intentional in drawing near to them and allowing them to encourage me.

Your Personal Worth

The women said to Naomi:
". . . For your daughter-in-law, who loves you and who is better to you than seven sons, has given him birth."

Ruth 4:14-15

*W*hat an amazing and insightful statement from Naomi's female friends. True, these words of praise for Ruth were not voiced until after the birth of her son. But there is truth within them that needs emphasis.

In the Jewish culture, the affirmation of a woman's value came not only through her attachment to a man (since men were usually seen as the civic, legal, and economic leaders), but through the fruitfulness of her womb, and more specifically if she could produce male children. Women were shamed by their husbands and often divorced by them if they could not bear children. Yet these wise women in the book of Ruth affirmed a truth that God had spoken in the beginning, when he said that he would make human beings to be "like himself," both male and female. (Genesis 1:26-27) To God, women and men are valuable because we were all created to be like him and to have fellowship with him. Naturally there was not one indication from God that he would value some women over others because of their ability to birth children.

But even these Jewish women, steeped as they were in their culture's value system, declared that for Naomi to have Ruth, a loving woman to watch over her, to accompany her, and to provide for her, had been of much more value than seven sons (who might not have been nearly as loving or as caring). With these words they not only encouraged the new grandmother (to stop mourning her husband and sons and give due credit to the wonderful woman God had placed beside her), but they also encouraged Ruth, the new mother. They affirmed her as a whole and valuable person, loving and good, irrespective of the fact that she had just given birth to a male child.

Reflecting

1. Consider who you were as a person *before* you became "the mother of . . . " or even "the wife of . . . "
2. Recall former words spoken to you that affirmed your personhood, your qualities, your gifts, or your contribution to the lives of others. Write them in your journal.
3. Call another woman today and affirm who she is and what she means to you.

Praying

Thank you, God, that you see me as a complete, valued person, made in your image, irrespective of motherhood. From that creation comes my value, my source of being. Help me to be sensitive to and give full value to women (as your created daughters) who for varied and multiple reasons are unable to birth children. Help me to share my child with them.

79

"She Did What She Could"

"Leave her alone," said Jesus. "Why are you bothering her? She has done a beautiful thing to me. . . . She did what she could."

Mark 14:6-8

*P*arenting a little one at best is overwhelming—overwhelming in the emotion, time, energy, and decision making it takes. Did you ever imagine that one so tiny, so longed for and sought after, could be so intrusive in every area of your life? Day or night, with no regard for people, venue, or time, the feeding, diapering, and consoling *must* take place. The little one demands, expects, and needs these regularly—and *irregularly,* it may seem to us!

In the heat of all this, you may begin to wonder who you are, what you have to give, and *how* you're supposed to give it. Your mind may take you to a helpful book you've read or more likely replay a role model that you have seen or heard talk about this situation and how to deal with it.

But don't forget that you are *you.* And no one understands that better than the Lord Jesus Christ, your Creator. In the above Scripture, Mary of Bethany annointed Jesus with very costly perfume, much to the astonishment and voiced horror of the men sitting with the Savior. To them, she gave the wrong gift in the wrong way at the wrong time. To Jesus, Mary's giving was exactly right. Why? Because Jesus knew *she had given what she could*—at the right time and in the right way.

I have wished in some areas that I could have given more and differently to my children. At times I have even allowed myself to be devastated when I compared my style of parenting with that of others who gave what I could not. You will give to your child some of what your parents gave you, but much of what you give will come innately from you, something your parents could not give. Your children will pass on some of you, but much of what they will give your grandchildren will be those beautifully distinct gifts given to them by their Creator, which you did not have.

If you are tempted to be overwhelmed today with feelings of inadequacy, step back and remember that in spite of others' condemnation and misperception, Jesus affirmed Mary. "She has done a beautiful thing to me . . . *she did what she could.*"

Reflecting

1. How do you see yourself mothering differently from your role models?
2. What do you have, within yourself, that they do not?

Praying

Loving God, thank you for reminding me that I have been uniquely made by you—and you are beside me in my mothering. Give me patience with those who do not understand me and with those I find hard to understand.

Willingness and Courage

*A*s new moms, willingness and courage are often the essential traits we need. The following woman's story involves not only a major move, but an *abnormal* challenge as well.

Ever heard of Zipporah? Now *there's* a courageous new mom! Zipporah was Moses' dark-skinned, Midianite wife.

For Moses, failure came before fame. Having just killed an Egyptian, he ran for his life. His rest stop by a desert well one day was short-lived when he jumped to his feet to defend Zipporah and her six sisters from a band of macho shepherds.

And thus began the nomadic romance of Zipporah and Moses. They married, had son Gershom, *and* a routine. You can just imagine Zipporah trying to keep sand out of the tent, cooking over an open fire, weaving, washing clothes, taking care of their child, visiting with her clan, and enjoying the closeness and strange ideas of her Israelite-Egyptian husband. Meanwhile, Moses chased after the family sheep and goats.

Then God called Moses to deliver a nation. What did this mean for Zipporah? It meant leaving her entire support system. It meant monstrous change, shattered routine, hard travel, plunging into an unknown culture of unfriendly people, and myriads of other uncertainties. Yet the biblical narrative indicates no

So Moses took his wife and sons, put them on a donkey, and started back to Egypt.

Exodus 4:20

hesitation on her part. To further complicate things—and this underscores the courage of Zipporah—she carried with her a new baby boy, Eliezer.

Just days into the journey to Egypt, things went wrong. Perhaps it was because of worries about the great task before him and the arduous trip that Moses forgot. But God didn't. Moses failed in his responsibility to circumcise Eliezer on the eighth day after birth. God himself would now take Moses' life because of his disobedience. Was all lost? No, because Zipporah stepped forward and with calm strength circumcised her son.

Though the customs are different from our own today, we can take heart from Zipporah's strengths: first, her willingness as a new mom to move when God called, although it meant leaving what she knew and loved; and second, her courage to do something radically different, outside her comfort zone.

Can you imagine the Old Testament without Moses, without the first five books, which he wrote? Thank God for the willingness and calm courage of Zipporah!

Reflecting   How do you see God refining the quality of courage in your life through motherhood?

Praying   Loving God, give me courage today to willingly follow you.

Weaning

My heart is not proud, O LORD, my eyes are not haughty; I do not concern myself with great matters or things too wonderful for me. But I have stilled and quieted my soul; like a weaned child with its mother, like a weaned child is my soul within me.

Psalm 131:1-2

Some babies and their moms wean well. For others weaning can be a painful experience, both physically and emotionally. Weaning all three of our children was never the idyllic experience I had envisioned. Each time brought distinct joys and discomforts.

Our first child nursed for nine months and went straight to a cup. I was skinnier than a stick and worried that our baby would become sick like the babies surrounding us in the Peruvian jungle. But, fat and happy, she seemed to thrive on it all. Our second child had to be weaned literally in one day, when I became deathly ill. It was a difficult time for him as well as for me. As for our third child, I was never certain if I had enough milk and finally weaned her at four months, when she began to adjust to a bottle. The second and third children also lived and were healthy! Only *I* wrestled with feelings of guilt and sadness.

A pleasant remembrance remains for all three—weaning means a greater degree of independence for both baby and mother, and as the Scripture indicates, a greater degree of quietness and rest in each other's presence. Your body signals are not screaming to feed that child, nor is the child pawing you to be fed! *Celebrate!*

You may be preparing for a change of schedule—perhaps going back to work outside the home, finding a part-time caregiver for your little one. Whatever the pending change, keep yourself before the Lord as a "weaned child," quiet, still, at peace with him, because you know you can trust him. Your child does not concern himself with the future. That is something he can't yet comprehend. But he will trust the one who feeds him today. Likewise, you will not be able to fit all the pieces of the future together at this moment either—work, daycare, relationships, expenses, other goals, etc. But you *can* be quiet before God, taking one step at a time, trusting him for the future.

Reflecting

1. How would you identify your relationship with God today—as a weaned child, quiet and trusting, or otherwise? In your journal, explain the feelings you have.
2. Why not share these thoughts with your husband or another person close to you. Talk together about trust, the future, and your mutual feelings about how to treat it.

Praying

Dear Creator, I want to be like a weaned child before you. Help me not to worry over what I cannot control, but begin to take one step at a time forward with you.

Like Mother, Like . . . ?

*God heard
Manoah, and the
angel of God
came again to
the woman while
she was out in
the field; but her
husband Manoah
was not with her.*

Judges 13:9

*T*he Bible does not name every godly mother. So it is with Judge Samson's mother.

Although we do not know her name or family background, nor the social stigma and inner pain she bore because she could not bear children, her spirit of obedience to God is praiseworthy. Against this dark, violent period of Israelite history, Mrs. Manoah sparkles like a freshly polished diamond. Her faithfulness to God is so evident that the Invisible chooses to communicate directly with her instead of with her husband, Manoah.

Again the themes of pregnancy, childbearing, and childrearing bring a woman face to face with her Maker. The angel of the Lord appears to her. Spiritually perceptive, she recognizes him as such. Considering her responsible, the angel gives her specific health instructions to follow throughout her pregnancy, guidelines for rearing this special child, and a view of her son's future career. She believes the angel of the Lord. The ensuing scenes between her, Manoah, and the reappearing angel (conceding to Manoah's plea) only underscore the calm maturity, faith, and wisdom of this woman. And later, she does give birth and names her son Samson.

But Samson's story does not read like a well-honed fairy tale with a "happily ever after" ending. It doesn't even read like a modern Christian novel, where God often makes things cheery in the last chapter. No, Samson's story would break any godly mother's heart. But would it shake her trust in God?

From all Scriptural evidence, Mrs. Manoah continued down the path of belief in the goodness of the Living God, even as she watched her son confront the wickedness of the times and often become engulfed by it.

Perhaps the greatest lesson from this story is that a mother's godliness does not guarantee the godliness of a child. Nor should a godly parent allow the ungodliness of an adult child to cast doubt on God's character or goodness. Mrs. Manoah fulfilled her responsibility to God and to her son. It was Samson's responsibility to build on the godly lessons she had given him.

Reflecting

1. What do you want to transmit to your child about God?
2. What has been your response to godly parents of wandering children?

Praying

Loving God, guide me in the teaching of this precious child. Help me to really trust you with her as the years march on.

Letting Go

Children are a blessing and a gift from the LORD. Having a lot of children to take care of you in your old age is like a warrior with a lot of arrows.

Psalm 127:3-4, CEV

*I*n the Bible children are considered neither an economic drain nor an obstacle to social life. They are regarded as a welcome blessing from God's creative hand.

One reason they are seen as a blessing is described in the word picture of Psalm 127. As arrows were used by warriors in offense tactics, so children would grow and be present to defend their parents in war and in legal strife. Those without family, such as widows and orphans, were taken advantage of.

However, consider the value of an arrow if it is never pulled out of the quiver, never placed in the bow and launched into the air, never sent out to accomplish the goal for which it was made, always kept tucked inside close to the owner—"of such value," one might say, "that I just can't let it go."

Think of Jochebed and Moses. What if she had said, "Look, a person suffers so much in the carrying and bearing of a child. This child is unique and the youngest. I am *not* going to let him out of my sight." Who would have delivered the Israelites from the Egyptians?

Then there's Hannah and Samuel, who left her side to become prophet, priest, and judge in Israel. In spite of Hannah's suffering over her inability to have children, she did not threaten

God, "Give me a child or I'll die," as had her foremother Rachel. She said, "Give me a child, God, and I'll give him back to you."

Letting go of our children is never easy. The process was no easier for Mary, the mother of Jesus. Undoubtedly, along with the awe she experienced upon hearing Simeon's prophecy came also a wince of pain when he directed toward her the words "and a sword will pierce your own soul, too." Jesus was no more than six weeks old.

Too soon, you say, to consider letting go of this little one? No, it is never too soon to pray over the future of your child, to ask for grace and trusting heart to one day allow this gift, this reward, this arrow to dismiss itself from the quiver, to glide *with your blessing* into that place God has chosen. Only in this way will the arrow willingly return to you, and you both will once again embrace—full of joy, full of peace—friends.

Reflecting

What are two positive steps you can take to remind yourself that this child is in your care only for a time?

Praying

Loving God, thank you for releasing your only son, Jesus. May my hands and heart remain open to your example and direction in the parenting of my child.

Like a Child

*W*e held our breath. Three-year-old Brandon, a bundle of great energy and enthusiasm, took ten steps back into the kitchen, charged across the hall, and hurled himself out into mid-air over nine steep steps. An eternity later he landed safely below—in Grandpa's waiting arms! Low whistles of relief and admiration escaped our lips. But the stunt *had* to be repeated—again and again *and again* until Grandpa (*not* Brandon!) begged for a rest.

A little child . . . such unadulterated trust, such humility, such vulnerability.

In today's Scripture, can't you see the little child Jesus had called forward, leaning shyly but securely against Jesus' leg or resting in the curve of his arm, peering curiously yet confidently up at the big adult disciples who surrounded him? Unlike most teachers and writers of the ancient world, who saw children as completely insignificant, Jesus loved little children.

He welcomed them. He held them on his lap. He blessed them with gracious words and actions. He went out of his way to heal them. He considered service rendered to them by his disciples as service rendered to himself. Jesus loved little children.

Jesus still loves little children. He loves yours. And he considers the service you render to your little one as service rendered directly to him! Amazing and reassuring, isn't it? This little one you hold—so trusting, so humble, so vulnerable—has become a very present avenue for serving God, for welcoming God himself anew into your life and home.

Reflecting

1. In what ways is your baby teaching you to be more childlike in your approach to God?
2 What new feelings and thoughts toward small children have been stirred within you since having your own child?

Praying

Creator God, today I thank you for your deep love and respect for all small children, including mine. Thank you for seeing my service to my precious child as service to you. Please remind me of that, Lord, when I grow weary.

The Promise of the Future

Then our sons in their youth will be like well-nurtured plants, and our daughters will be like pillars carved to adorn a palace.

Psalm 144:12

*W*ell-nurtured *plants*—healthy and growing, bringing glory to God. Carved *pillars* adorning a palace—strong and upright, turning others' eyes heavenward. What creative word pictures King David used to describe the kind of children he desired for the nation of Israel. Now, several thousand years later, have our desires changed for our children? Probably not much.

You look down at the little one you hold, and of course you desire the very best for her. But sometimes, in the muddle of sleeplessness, crying, and a new routine, we can unwittingly feel that the whole outcome of this new life rests on *our* thin shoulders. In a saner moment, we need to consider what we can do and what we may not be able to do—what we have control of and what we do not have control of. Surely every mom has high hopes for her child, but not every hope has been realized.

Consider the spectrum of women to whom children are born: some are on a career track; others are peasants. Some are mentally sound; others live emotionally unstable. Some have healthy homes; others live in unwelcoming hovels. Or consider the environments into which the baby arrives: some come under repressive governments; others into full freedom. Some are born into war situations, others into peace. Some are born in concentration camps, ghettos, or refugee hostels; others are welcomed into protected middle-class suburbs. For many of us, life reflects our choices; yet for thousands more, much of life is outside our control. That still does not limit a mother's hopes and dreams for her child.

And God, our loving God, moving among us, is near you. He is aware of your strengths and limitations, your hopes and dreams for this child. Pray for your child, love her, provide for her, and guide her. And God will work with you. With God beside you, what you now consider a disadvantage for your child may well be turned into an advantage.

Reflecting

1. What do you consider sensible goals that you might desire for your child? What could be some fantasies?
2. As you consider the first three years of your child's life, make a small list in your journal of those things which you can possibly control and other items which realistically are outside of your control.

Praying

Lord, help me today to do what I can for my baby and leave what is not possible for me with you. May I be at peace with what you have given me for this day.

On to Other Business

*P*erhaps it's been several weeks or months since you birthed. You may now be considering other business alongside the mothering of your little one. Some women choose to remain at home. Others are also able to generate an income from this home base. Many, however, are obliged to provide an income and can only accomplish that through work outside the home.

The last twenty-one verses of Proverbs were not written to discourage and confuse us by presenting a one-woman super heroine, charging from manager to seamstress, from lecturer to volunteer worker among the poor, from home supervisor to real estate agent! Rather, it should be considered as a collage or sampling of the many gifts and open doors for women, arranged in a Hebrew acrostic poem.

Throughout the seemingly frenetic activity of this poem moves stable, focused womanhood, working intently, arduously to be *responsible*—responsible to God, to family, and to society.

Being responsible, which involves setting biblical priorities and making the necessary choices, is never easy. For all of us it involves struggle and hard work. And your outworking of responsibility may not look like your friend's. But as you seek God for guidance and godly friends for wisdom in the integra-

Let her works bring her praise at the city gate.

Proverbs 31:31

tion of your baby's needs alongside your own continued development, if necessary at a limited pace, you will find answers to your needs: peace and joy in responsibility.

One day, with God and you working together, your works also—mothering, wifing, and developing and using your God-given gifts—will rise up to praise you!

Reflecting

1. What are two major changes occurring in your life right now? What person or persons can be helpful to you in making decisions concerning these changes?
2. To what acts of responsibility do you sense God is calling you as you consider these changes?

Praying

Loving God, I thank you for your awareness of my life today—of my baby's needs as well as my own. I praise you for the answers you are going to give me as I present to you those needs. Thank you for giving me the strength and creativity to be a responsible woman before you, my family, and society.